BASQUE COUNTRY

Euskal Herria

ESVS·MARIA
TRISTANT
DHARGINDE
MARIA D
FRANCE
TEGVI

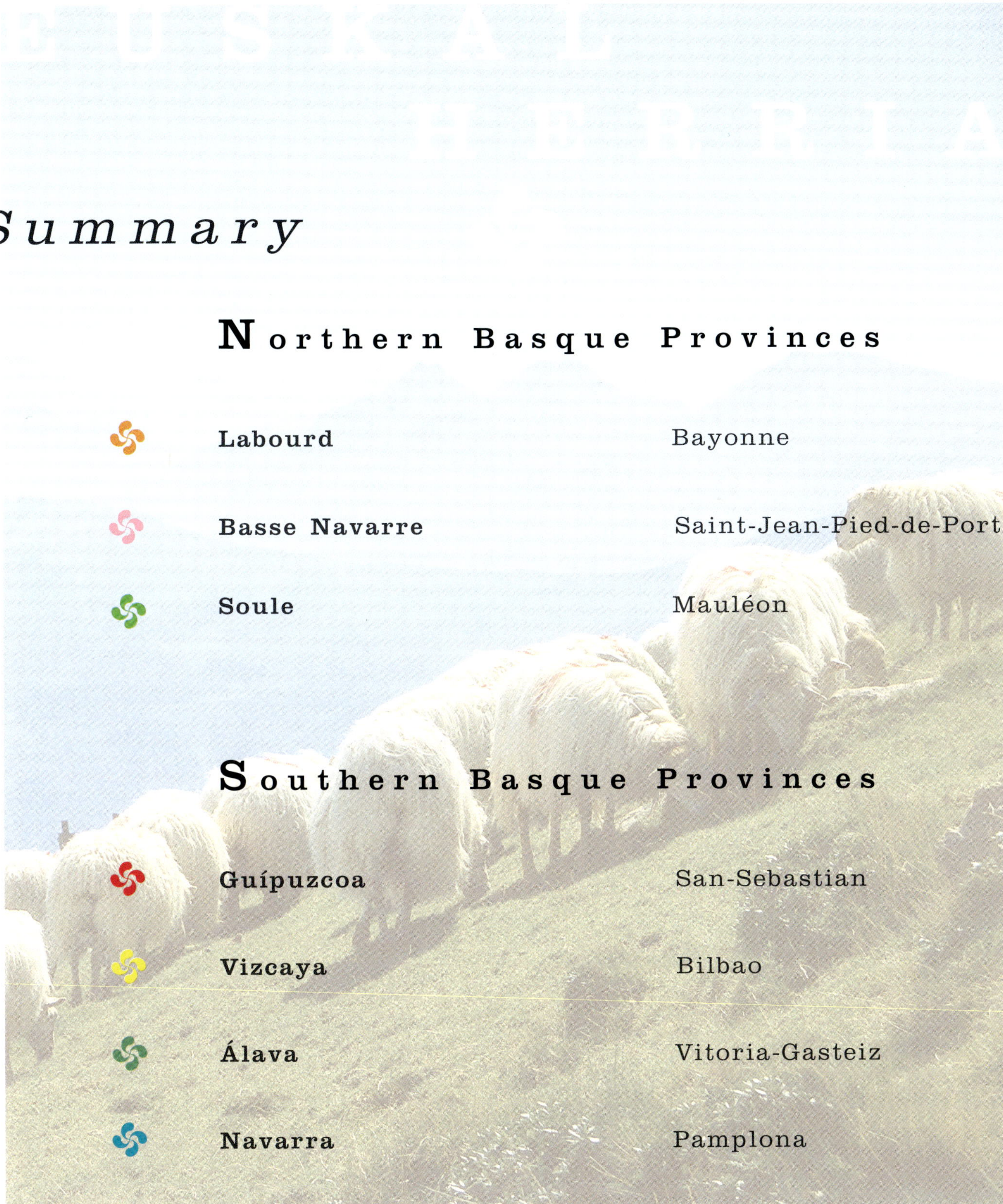

Summary

Northern Basque Provinces

Labourd	Bayonne
Basse Navarre	Saint-Jean-Pied-de-Port
Soule	Mauléon

Southern Basque Provinces

Guípuzcoa	San-Sebastian
Vizcaya	Bilbao
Álava	Vitoria-Gasteiz
Navarra	Pamplona

Labourd

BAYONNE - BAïONA

Aerial view of Bayonne at the confluence of the Nive and Adour rivers

In the 5th century Bayonne was a Roman stronghold known under the name Lapurdum. The city is situated on the confluence of the Adour and Nive rivers.
In the 9th century it was invaded by the Vikings who were in their turn chased out a century later by the Duke of Gascony, Sanche Guillaume.
In 1152 the city came under English domination through the marriage between Alienor d'Aquitaine and Henry II Plantagenet. In the 11th century it got the name Baiona. Up until the 16th century the Adour river flowed out further north, in the Landes.
Bayonne is also a military city and fortifications were built here until the 19th century.
The city is divided into three main districts : Grand Bayonne, Petit Bayonne and Saint-Esprit. The Pont Saint-Esprit, which spans the Adour, was first built of wood in 1125. It was much appreciated by the pilgrims who needed to cross the river on their way to Santiago de Compostela. This bridge linked the city to the Saint-Esprit district which was then reserved for Jews. The Jews had an important role in the economic activity in the city and it was most probably they who first brought chocolate to Bayonne. It remains one of the city's specialities.
The Citadel was built in 1680 by Vauban.
The Saint-Esprit church has been altered several times over the centuries. It has a remarkable polychrome wood sculpture representing the Flight into Egypt.

GRAND BAYONNE
The construction of the Sainte-Marie or Notre-Dame cathedral started in the 13th century. It was seriously

The cloister

damaged during the revolution. The two spires and the sacristy were built at the end of the 19th century. The cloister was a meeting place of the trades and a burial place for the dignitaries.
The Place Pasteur was the old public square where the pillory stood, on the site of the present fountain.
The Château-Vieux is a square fortress built in the 17th century on top of two towers from the ancient Roman ramparts. The Rue Thiers is the old Rue des Tanneries and many houses in this street have tannery pits in their basements. The city is enclosed within its ramparts and a large population increase caused an urbanization problem, which explains why the houses were heightened by several floors.
Some of these houses have magnificent Gothic cellars that were used as storage rooms to protect merchandise from fire. Guided visits of these cellars are now organised. The Rue Port-Neuf, one of the most picturesque streets in Bayonne, was built in the 16th century on the site of a canal. There are plenty of shops under its arcades and several of them sell the city's famous chocolate.
The quay houses are built on piles and consist of two main parts separated by a small central court lit up by a glassroof.

PETIT BAYONNE

A local merchant built the Maison Dagorette in the 16th century with large harbour storage facilities. It was later turned into a convent of the Order of the Visitation and after that it was a hospital until the time of the Second Empire. In 1924 it was turned into a museum, the Musée Basque, dedicated to the history and culture of the Basque people.
The Château-Neuf fortress with its large circular towers and small courtyard was finished in 1462. It dominates the historical part of Bayonne and helped controlling the left bank of the Adour, the fortified Mousserolles

The King Léon on the town hall balcony during the Fêtes de Bayonne

gate and the access-ways to the city. The famous Fêtes de Bayonne cow running takes place in the Place Saint-André.
Pelote Basque (a ball game) is played in the old Jeu de Paume court in the Rue du Trinquet.
The Saint-André church was built between 1856 and 1869. The Musée Bonnat holds more than 5000 works of art. The Rue Pannecau is one of the oldest streets in Petit Bayonne and it is also one of the liveliest streets in the city at night.

THE FÊTES DE BAYONNE

The King Léon opens the fêtes from the town hall balcony on the first Wednesday of August at 10pm with a concerto of fireworks, "la mascleta".
The fêtes goes on, day and night, until the following Sunday with cow running on the Place Saint André, parade of carts, children's day, Sunday bullfight, Basque dancing "mutxikoak", bandas, public dances, toros de fuego and thousands of "festayres" dressed in white with red scarf and belt.

THE BULLFIGHT

The first ever bullfight in France took place in the Saint-Esprit arena on 21 August 1853. The Lachepaillet arena was inaugurated in 1893. From July to September crowds of aficionados come here.

THE HAM

The ham owes its name to the port of Bayonne from where it was shipped out all over Europe. The ham came from the surrounding countryside and was cured with the famous salt from the Adour valley. It was introduced to the Royal court thanks to Henri IV.

The quays along the Nive and Petit Bayonne

ANGLET - ANGELU

Between the mouth of the Adour and the Biarritz lighthouse there are more than four kilometres of fine sandy beaches that attract the best surfers in the world: the beaches La Barre, Cavaliers, Océan, Les Dunes Madrague, Corsaires, Sables d'Or and Chambre d'Amour.
The Brise-Lames marina, by the mouth of the Adour, hosts amateur fishing boats and yachts.
The Chiberta forest is a 250 hectare wooded area with pine trees offering numerous walks by its famous golf-course, its lake and beautiful villas. The Notre-Dame du Refuge convent, situated in this forest, was founded in 1839 with a mission to help reformed prostitutes through prayers and activities like cultivation and stock breeding.
The Chambre d'Amour's cave got its name from a legend of two young lovers who drowned inside the cave.
The town hall, built in 1939, is a beautiful example of Neo-Spanish style with patio, balconies and azulejos tile decor. It was designed by the architect Marcel who also designed the interior of the Château de Brindos.

By the beach, with the Biarritz lighthouse in the background

The Saint-Léon church was built in 1583 then altered in the 17th century. It has a double row of galleries. Over the last few years Anglet has seen the development of industrial parks and shopping areas. This very vast commune links Bayonne and Biarritz. A lazaret was built on the dunes along the Adour at the end of the 16th century and it served for sanitary control of the ships and quarantine for contagious diseases.

The Pointe St Martin and the beaches

The Chambre d'Amour's cave

BIARRITZ - MIARRITZE

The Grande Plage and the Hôtel du Palais

The Villa Belza

Biarritz has been known since prehistoric times. It was a fishing port situated by the present Port-Vieux beach until 1790, when a new fishing port was built. Biarritz was famous for its whaling already in the 12th century. Seawater baths became popular here at the end of the 18th century. Thanks to the visits of the empress Eugénie de Montijo and Napoleon III this fishing village became the place to be for the rich and famous. Biarritz was developed with the constructions of different architectural styles that today gives it its charm. Many writers stayed here, Victor Hugo, Flaubert, Sacha Guitry....as well as aristocracy from all over the world. The lighthouse on the Pointe St Martin was built in 1834. It is 44m high and reaches 73m above the sea level. The Imperial couple had the Villa Eugénie, the present Hôtel du Palais, built in 1854. The building has three main parts and is built in the shape an E. It had a floor added onto it before it was sold to the town in 1881 and transformed into a hotel-casino.
The Saint Alexandre Nievski Orthodox church was built

at the end of the 19th century by the town's Russian colony, which was very large at the time.
The imposing Miramar hotel, situated on the beach with the same name, was transformed into a hotel-thalassotherapy spa.
The Art Deco-style casino set on the Grande plage was built in 1924.
The Bellevue casino was changed into a Second Empire and Art Deco-style and stood finished in 1950.
In 1905, on the empress Eugénie's initiative, the Sainte-Eugénie church replaced the chapel built on the site in 1856.
The Atalaye plateau offers a fantastic view of the southern coast, of the charming fishing port below with its "crampotes", tiny fishermen's houses, and of the rocher du Basta with its natural arc. La tour de la Humade once stood here. It was a tower on top of which wet straw was burnt in order to announce the arrival of the whales.
A footbridge built under Gustave Eiffel's supervision stretches over to the rocky islet, Rocher du Cucurlon or Rocher de la Vierge (Rock of the Virgin). It takes its name from statue crowning it since 1865. The ocean, whether calm or rough, offers a fantastic scenery. From the lighthouse to the Côte de Basque beach you can enjoy it by day as well as by night thanks to a very beautiful artificial illumination. The Art Deco-style Musée de la Mer was built in 1933. It has numerous aquariums of fish but it also houses sharks. Visitors can watch the feeding of the seals twice a day.
The Port-Vieux, old port, where in the past the whales were brought and then flensed, has a small beach offering calm and nice swimming conditions.
The Villa Belza, finished in 1895, housed a Russian cabaret during the roaring twenties. It overlooks the Côte des Basques beach from its rock. This beach was given its name because of the Basque people who came here to swim every Sunday following the Assumption.
All along the seafront there are paths and lovely walks where it is nice to enjoy the calm and dream away on a bench.
The old train station, built in Arudy stone, is now a convention centre.
The recently renovated Saint-Martin church was built in the 12th century and restored in 1541. It has a Flamboyant Gothic chancel. The very first houses in Biarritz were built around this church.

The Rocher de la Vierge, the Musée de la Mer and the Port-Vieux

The Rocher de la Vierge

The Port des Pêcheurs and the Rocher du Basta

The Imperial chapel, dedicated to the black Mexican Virgin Notre-Dame de Guadalupe, was built in 1864 of brick and stone, in a combination of Romanesque-Byzantine and Hispano-Moorish styles. Its interior is very richly decorated.
Several nice walks have been laid out by Lake Marion and you can also enjoy a stroll around Lake Mouriscot in the Negresse district.
Every year there are plenty of conferences, surfing competitions and festivals with different themes organised in Biarritz ; cinema, audiovisual, dance, theatre and music. The fireworks, shot off from the Grande plage and the rocks around it, on 15 August every year mark the peak of the summer season.
The beaches of Marbella and Milady as well as Ilbarritz, with the Château du Baron de l'Espée, are situated south of Biarritz.
Ilbarritz golf training centre is the largest one in Europe.

Aquarium in the Musée de la Mer

The Côte de Basque beach

ARCANGUES - ARRANGOITZE

This charming village exists since the 12th century. The Château d'Arcangues, rebuilt in the 19th century, is still the home of the Marquis d'Arcangues. Wellington set up his headquarters here in 1814, during the battles of the Nive.
Walking through the village you will discover the school and the town hall with their typical Arcangues-blue shutters, the fronton and the Auberge with its shale tables. The church was built at the end of the 12th century and it has magnificent 18th century galleries made of sculptured wood. It also holds a bas relief representing the beheading of St John the Baptist, as well as golden altarpieces. Just below the village square is the "Théatre de la nature" and the Dolphin fountain surrounded by the seigneurial benches.
The cemetery surrounding the church has many typically Basque gravestones including that of Luis Mariano, a famous operette singer who died in 1970. This terraced site overlooks the panorama where one of the battles of the Nive was fought in 1814.

Luis Mariano's grave

The Presbytery with the bell tower in the background

Church's interior

BIDART - BIDARTE

The beach seen from la Madeleine

Bidart is an old whaling port set on the pilgrims' route to Compostela. It is today a small seaside resort with houses decorated with "sang-de-boeuf"red half-timberings, a square and town hall, "herriko etxea", a fronton and a church. The Notre-Dame de l'Assomption church was built in the 16th century and has a fortified bell tower. It houses a wooden statue of St James dressed like a pilgrim, a Serbo-Croatian baptistmal font donated by Queen Nathalie of Serbia, and a Baroque altarpiece. The Sainte-Madeleine chapel, where unidentified seamen were buried, was rebuilt in the 19th century. It is situated in a conservation area and offers a fantastic view of the Cantabrian coast and the Pyrenees. The Notre-Dame d'Uronea chapel, "la bonne eau", holds an 18th century Virgin Mary sculpture made of golden wood. The water from the spring situated on this site was famous for curing skin diseases.

The Saint-Joseph chapel set above the Parlamentia beach was reserved for lepers.

The dethroned Queen Nathalie of Serbia once lived in the Domaine de Sachino, which is today a royal pavilion.

The town hall

The Uhabia river flows out into the ocean just south of the village. The Bassilour mill from 1741 is still in use. A wheel turns the millstones giving an old fashioned flour used by the miller to make bread, loafs, biscuits and the famous gateau Basque.

GUETHARY - GETARIA

Sunset on the harbour with the Trois Couronnes in the background

Pelote players (pelotari) in front of the town hall

Guéthary, situated between the Uhabia and the Baldareta rivers, is a very old village with remains of a 1st century Roman settlement. In 1193 it was a fishing village known under the name Catari. The lighthouse, a former "atalaye" or whale-watch tower, is the only one left on the coast.

The 17th century Saint-Nicolas church with its three floors of galleries is the highest point in the village and serves as a landmark for seamen.

The museum set up in the fantastic Neo-Basque Villa Saraleguinea has collections of Roman remains, works of the Romanian sculptor Sviecinski as well as contemporary artworks.

One of the highest frontons in the Basque Country is set on the village's Neo-Basque style town hall square. The beaches in Guéthary are a paradise for surfers.

ST JEAN-DE-LUZ - DONIBANE LOHITZUN

The Interior of the Saint Jean-Baptiste church

Aerial view of the bay

St Jean-de-Luz was a fishing port already in prehistoric times. From the 10th century the whaling made the town prosperous and this lasted until the Middle Ages when this cetacean became rare and the fishermen had to follow it far north. The 17th century saw the decline of this fishing as well as the salt cod fishing and the fishermen now focused on sardines and tuna.

In the 18th century parts of the town were destroyed by terrible storms and breakwaters were constructed in1827, on order by Napoleon III. A large number of Basque corsaires (privateers) scoured the seas between the 16th and 19th centuries. At the end of the 19th century St Jean-de-Luz became a seaside resort. The Maison Louis XIV (also called Maison Lohobiague) was built in 1643 and got its name from the fact that the young Louis XIV stayed here during the preparations for his wedding, in June 1660, to the Spanish Infanta Maria-Teresa. His bride stayed not far from

The fishing port and the Maison de l'Infante

there in the Maison de l'Infante. The shaded Place Louis XIV, its many open air cafés and its pavilion are surrounded by beautiful houses, like the town hall, finished in 1657. A statue of Louis XIV has a place of honor in the middle of the u-formed building.
The port, dating back to the 12th century, harbours the fishingboats and it becomes very busy when the fishermen bring back their catch of tuna, anchovies and sardines. The Rue de la République is a busy street with plenty of restaurants serving marmitako, tuna ragout with potatoes ; koskera hake ; piballes, eel juveniles or elvers ; ttoro, a local fishsoup ; chipirons or baby squid ; tuna kaskarotte, and for sweet lovers ; the delicious macaroons, invented in the 17th century by the pâtissier Adam who made the young King Louis XIV try them. The church of Jean-Baptiste was destroyed by a fire and then rebuilt and altered until the 19th century. The wedding of Louis XIV was celebrated here in 1660 and the door through which the royal couple left the church was walled up in 1669. Inside, the church has a single nave, three floors of galleries and a magnificent 17th century altarpiece decorated with an abundance of statues. There is an 18th century stairway with a magnificent wrought iron banister on the outside of the church.

Rue de la République

The bay

The seafront is lined with houses in various styles and the casino, which also houses a thalassotherapy spa. The Pointe Sainte-Barbe with its beautiful Basque villas offers a fantastic panorama of the bay and the mountains.
Several cultural festivals take place in the town every year : classical concerts, dance, theatre, choral singing, music.

Fishing boats

Maison Louis XIV

CIBOURE - SOCOA - URRUGNE - IBARDIN

The quay Ravel

CIBOURE-SOCOA - ZUBIBURE-ZOKOA

Ciboure is situated on the other side of the Nivelle and was originally a part of Urrugne. Because of its location far from St Jean-de-Luz and Urrugne it became a refuge for adventurers and other people living on the fringe of society : the "cagots" (lepers and their descendants), bohemians, Jews and Moors. This mix of people became the "cascarot" population. The local women went all the way to Bayonne to sell the sardines their men caught.
Maurice Ravel was born in a superb Flemish-style house built of dressed stones with gables and gargoyles in the shape of canons, witnessing of the existing connection with the Nordic countries. The town hall, built in 1720, is surrounded by beautiful houses and a fountain from 1676 stands on its square. The Saint-Vincent church was built in the 16th century and enlarged in the 17th century. It has an octogonal bell tower with a wooden structure that is unique in the Basque Country. The Récollets convent was founded in 1612. Today only the cloister and a fountain donated by Mazarin remain. Pierre Benoit, a 19th century writer who lived and died in Bordagain, is buried in its cemetery. The 82-metre high Bordagain tower was used as a lookout post. The magnificent Leihorra, Itzala and Lehentokia villas are examples of constructions developed during the roaring twenties. The construction of the Socoa fort started in 1627 and it was later reinforced by Vauban. It was built according to the wishes of Henri IV. Its large round tower dominates a cliff with impressive layers of sediment.

The Socoa's Fort

URRUGNE-URRUNA

Urrugne was originally one of the biggest parishes in the Labourd province. In the centre of the village, in front of the old post house, stands the austere fortified Saint Vincent de Xaintes church. It was built in the 16th century and altered in the 19th century, and it holds a holy-water basin for cagots.
The Notre-Dame de Socorri chapel was built on the top of a hill according to the wishes of grateful seamen. It is surrounded by disc-shaped engraved steles.
The Château d'Urtubie was fortified in 1341 and then altered several times due to the damage caused during invasions. It still belongs to the same family and is now open for visits and accommodation.
The Kalbario oratory close to Biriatou, where a calvary once stood, was destroyed in 1793 and a small chapel was built in its place.
Biriatou is a calm and green listed village set on the Xoldogaina hill overlooking the Bidassoa.
A number of historical events have taken place on the île des Faisans, "konpatzia" ; the 1469 meeting between Louis XI and Henri IV of Castille ; Isabelle of France met Anne of Austria here in 1615 and the signing of the Pyrenean peace treaty, which led to Louis XIV's engagement, took place here in 1659.

A road leads to the Ibardin col from where there is a superb view of the sea and the mountains. Plenty of "ventas", Spanish shops, sell Spanish products, cigarettes and alcohol at low prices.

Ibardin col

Urrugne

HENDAYE - HENDAIA

Aerial view of the bay with Spain in the background

The beach and the casino

The corniche road that links Socoa and Hendaye offers a fantastic panorama.
Hendaye was originally a hamlet in the parish of Urrugne. Pilgrims going to Compostela were welcomed in the Saint Jacques de Zubermoa priory as early as in the 12th century. It was a marshy area ; Vauban had a fortress built here that was destroyed by the Spanish at the end of the 18th century. The Saint-Vincent church looks just like a museum with its altar-pieces, statues, bas reliefs and paintings from the period between the 16th and 18th centuries, and its 13th century Christ and the baptismal font of which the basin is an old medieval holy water basin.
Due to its border-location Hendaye was often devastated.
The town was developed from 1864 thanks to the railway line and the opening of an international trainstation.

The Château d'Abbadia

The fashion of sea baths brought numerous holidaymakers to the town already back then. Hendaye-plage saw the construction of numerous hotels and villas as well as a sea bath establishment and a Neo-Moorish-style building on the seafront which housed a casino. This holidayresort is protected from the winds by the Jaizkibel Mountain and it is much appreciated for its long fine sandy beach and the small waves where children can safely play.
The twin rocks Deux Jumeaux stand in the sea in front of the Pointe de Sainte-Anne. The Château d'Abbadia, designed by Viollet-le-Duc, was built 1870 in a combination of Neo-Gothic and Oriental styles. This magnificently furnished castle shows a medieval influence with a donjon, towers and crenelles. It is today the property of the Académie des Sciences.
At one end of this beach are a thalassotherapy spa and a marina, set in the Txingudi bay.

Txingudi's bay

The Rochers des Deux Jumeaux

ASCAIN - AZKAINE

The village and its houses

A game of pelote and the Roman bridge

Ascain was referred to as early as 1125. The Nivelle runs through the village and it was on this river that the boats brought foods from St Jean de Luz.
On the square stands the fronton where a large number of pelotari come to play ; Pierre Loti wrote most of his novel "Ramuntcho", drawing inspiration from his friend the pelotari "Otharre", in the village.
The church was built at the end of the Middle Ages and had three floors of galleries added to it in the 17th century. Worth seeing in the church ; the altarpiece articulated by golden columns, the wooden ceiling, the gravestones, a medieval statue of Virgin Mary and Child and an ex-voto ship. The side door is said to be "reserved for cagots".
The town hall, in Louis XIII-style, is built of dressed stones. Large shipyards were once situated on the Nivelle. The "Roman" 17th century Uhertzia bridge with its three arches was washed away during the floods in 1993.

LA RHUNE - LARRUN

The top of La Rhune

The rack railway train

Since 1924 a small rack railway train ascends La Rhune from the St Ignace col. It reaches the top, at 905m altitude, in 30 minutes and from here you can enjoy a 360° panorama of the French and Spanish slopes and the Basque coast all the way to the beaches of the Landes. While ascending you will see pottoks, goats and sheep, as well as big vultures high above. Up until the revolution there was a Saint-Esprit chapel inhabited by a hermit, on top of La Rhune. This chapel was supposed to keep witches away.
The pink sandstone from La Rhune is used for framing windows and doorways. Driven into the ground these stones also serve as fencing in the fields.
There are still some protohistoric remains on La Rhune ; dolmens, tumulus and cromlech.

SARE - SARA

Sare is built against the foothills of La Rhune. It is set in green surroundings and benefits from a micro-climate. The Saint-Martin church was built in the 17th century. It is one of the most beautiful churches in the Labourd province with its five-floor, square bell tower, its medieval statue of Christ and gravestones on the floor. Discover the town hall and its lorio with five archways (lorio is a large porch in front of the houses in Labourd), the fronton and restaurants serving chicken basquaise, ringdove salmis, omelette with chili peppers and ewe milk cheese. This village has 14 oratories dedicated to various saints : Ste Barbe, St Antoine, St François-Xavier, St Michel, St Jean-Baptiste, St Pierre, St Isidore, St Nicolas, Ste Croix and St Ignace de Loyola. You can visit the Lezea cave and its large galleries hollowed out in the limestone by the waters rushing down from Mont Atchuria.
he smuggler's path links up the Sare caves to those in Urdax and Zuggaramurdi.

The village square and the church

Le Petit Paris

ST PEE SUR NIVELLE – SENPERE

Certain inscriptions in this village date back to the 13th century. The church, which was made higher in 1606, is paved with gravestones, with one dating back to1507. There are several galleries in the church and one of them was reserved for the nobility. The church houses a triple altarpiece and a choir with ribbed vaults. St Pee also has two chapels ; the Sainte Marie-Madeleine and the Sainte Barbe which was a place of pilgrimage. The oldest houses are situated in Ibarron and they have magnificent door lintels.
Only the Tour des Sorcières (Witch's tower) remains of the Château de Saint-Pee where Pierre de Lancre held witchcraft trials that sent hundreds of innocents to the stake at the beginning of the 17th century.
The mill, which belonged to the Seigneurs of Saint-Pee, was destroyed in 1449 by Gaston de Foix.
The specialities of Saint-Pee are the gateau Basque with cream or cherries, the taloa, a fried wheat and corn pancake that is served with ventrèche or cheese, and finally the delicious shortbreads.
The Saint-Pee forest stretches over 3500 hectare with mainly oak trees.
The lake and its banks have been designed for leisure activities and dolce farniente.

The Ibarron farm

The church's interior

The lake

AINHOA - AINHOA

Ainhoa is a fortified town founded at the end of the 12th century. It was a trade stopover on the road between Bayonne and Pamplona that runs through Batzan valley, as well as a stopping place for pilgrims on their way to Compostela. A castle, built by Juan Perez in the 13th century, once stood on the square on the site of the present fronton. The French-Spanish wars destroyed Ainhoa. The oldest remaining house was built before 1629. The rest of them were burnt down during the wars. The main street is lined with beautiful old houses with large lorios and green and red half-timberings.
The church, built in the 13th century, has loopholes and once served as refuge. It was altered in the 16th and 17th centuries and has very beautiful woodworks. On its cemetery stands tabular and disc-shaped steles.

The church's interior

Typical Labourd houses

The Notre-Dame d'Arantza chapel stands on the hill-side of the Atsula Mountain. In the 19th century a hermit taught the shepherds to read here.
The St Joseph chapel dates back to 1897.
In the 17th century Ainhoa had a mill that was collectively owned by the whole village. At the beginning of the 19th century another mill was built on the Opalazia stream. Ainhoa has several reputed restaurants and numerous artisans have settled in the village.
It is listed as one of the most beautiful villages in France.

ESPELETTE - EZPELETA

Espelette is situated by the Laxia and is made up of two areas, the castle and the church districts. The village inherited the Ezpeleta family castle, overlooking the Laxia stream, in the 17th century. This family's ancestors go back as far as the 11th century. Espelette had iron and kaolin mines.
The Saint-Etienne church was built in the 17th century with a solid bell tower, galleries and a Flemish-inspired 16th century altarpiece in the Ezpeleta chapel.
Espelette is famous for its piments, chili peppers, which decorate the facade of some of the village's white houses with garbles and corbelling. Both the mild and stronger chili peppers are used to prepare the axoa, based on minced veal, the chili pepper omelette, the piperade, the tripotxa, pork sausage and the tripaki, mutton sausage. The village is also famous for its pottoks, and the fair at the end of January is an event in the Basque Country.

The castle

The Ainhoa's church bell tower

Pottok's fair

Aerial view of Espelette

Ttipittoin Borda farm (drying of the chili peppers)

ITXASSOU - ITSASU

Itxassou is dominated by the Massifs of Mondarrin and Artzamendi. The Nive runs through the village which is arranged around the fronton and the typically Basque 17th century church. The church holds a 17th century treasure : cross, monstrance, chalice and ciborium. Its cemetery has several tabular and disc-shaped steles. Itxassou is renowned for its cherries and the famous black cherry jam made from them. This jam is savoured with the ewe milk cheese, ardi gasna, and used as filling for the gateau Basque.
A small road that links the village to the Arztamendi Massif goes through a huge rock that popular legend has named Pas de Roland (Roland's step), and then leads to the Laxia springs.
The Artzamendi Massif is 926 metres high and offers a fantastic panorama. It is possible to do hang gliding from the Mont Urzumu.

The Pas de Roland

General view

CAMBO - KANBO

Cambo-les-bains is built on a terrace overhanging the Nive. This thermal and health resort, famous since 1609, owes its name to its sulphurous and ferroginous thermal springs.
Edmond Rostand had "Arnaga", a vast Neo-Basque villa with a fantastic interior, built in the village. The villa and the French and English gardens with their superb ornamental ponds, orangery and "chanteclerc" farmyard, are open for visits. The Saint-Laurent church, altered several times, has a painting of the martyr Saint Laurent and three floors of galleries. A statue of Saint-Léon stands under its porch. The church is surrounded by lawns with disc-shaped steles.
Concerts are given on the square Albeniz, named after the musician who died in Cambo in 1909.
The Haslou church that holds a primitive style pièta and the Jatxou church with its primitive style Christ statue are situated in the vicinity.

Aerial view of the thermal spa

Aerial view of Cambo

Arnaga, Edmund Rostand's home

The big entrance hall

HASPARREN - HAZPARNE

The fronton and the church

The square

Hasparren used to be a stopping place for the St James pilgrims. This vast commune is divided into ten different areas scattered at the feet of the Monts Urtsuia and Baigura. The tanning industry and the production of chamois leather was greatly developed here from the 18th century on. The leather was exported as far as the Nordic countries and the shoes were sent out to the French colonies in America already in 1780.

Engraved stones from the 3rd century were discovered in the foundations of the church. Francis Jammes, a local boy, is buried in the cemetery in Hasparren. His house has been transformed into a museum and the garden is now a public park.

Aerial view of the square and the church

Francis Jammes' house

Basse Navarre

GROTTES D'ISTURITZ ET D'OXOCELHAYA

The Isturitz and Oxocelhaya caves are situated close to St Martin d'Arberoue. These caves are listed as ancient monuments and they are a reference in the research on prehistoric man.
The Arberoue river has hollowed out underground galleries that resemble a cathedral of rocks with monumental chalk stones, stalagmites and stalactites. These galleries were inhabited during thousands of years which the tools, bones and animal paintings found here prove.

A cave painting of a horse

Inside the caves

LABASTIDE-CLAIRENCE - BASTIDA

This fortified village was founded in 1312 by Louis le Hutin. The inhabitants were Gascons who built tissue mills for making cloth and leather. From the 18th century they worked in the nail and hosiery industries.
A Jewish colony settled in Labastide-Clairence in the 16th century and its cemetery still remains today.
This village has a fine architectural heritage : beautiful houses with archways and others with stone framing, the church with its 16th century Roman porch. Numerous artisans now work in the village : picture framers, ceramists, glassmakers, cabinetmakers, sculptors, weavers, painters, potter, upholsterers, mosaic makers, perfumers.

Navarra houses

SAINT-PALAIS – DONAPALEU

La Bidouze

Houses in Garris

The ruins of the Château de Gramont, which dates back to the 17th and 18th centuries, stand on a hill dominating the Bidouze river. There is a birds of prey aviary set up inside this castle.
A Royal Mint was built in the village in 1351 and it was in use until the 17th century.
Writings by numerous royal servants and the establishment of several inns witness of the important trade taking place in the village as early as in the 14th century. The Maison des têtes (the house of heads) with its five 17th century stone medallions is situated in the town centre, where the river la Joyeuse runs through. The stèle de Gibraltar stands by the road leading to Ostabat.

BIDARRAY – BIDARRAI

Bidarray was once a Roncesvalles priory and its chapel is today the village church. The church has been altered several times but the paving of its square still shows the Roncevalles coat of arms. You can cross the Nive by foot on the 14th century Pont Noblia. This three-arch bridge allowed the St James pilgrims to get across the river. The new bridge leads into the village. The Pont d'Enfer (Bridge of Hell) was rebuilt after the floods washed it away in 1913.
The Corpus Christi procession with the participation of sappers wearing fur hats, the village brass band and Basque dancers takes place in June.
Further along stands the cave of the "Saint-qui-sue"(the Saint that sweats). The drippings in this cave are supposed to cure skin diseases.

The Pont d'Enfer on the Nive

The church of pink sandstone

ST JEAN-PIED-DE-PORT – DONIBANE GARAZI

Houses on the Nive

St Jean-Pied-de-Port was founded at the end of the 12th century and it was quickly developed thanks to the stream of pilgrims passing through the village on their way to Santiago de Compostela. The pilgrims rested in the town's many inns and hospices before crossing the mountains and the Roncesvalles "pass" (col). King Sancho the Strong of Navarra turned St Jean-Pied-de-Port into a fortified town as early as in the 13th century. There are still the ogival doors, the Sainte-Eulalie d'Ugange church and the Notre-Dame church, called "du bout du pont", which has been altered several times. It is one of the most important Gothic constructions in the Basque Country. On the market square stands the Maison Mansart, a 17th century house built of dressed stones which today holds the town hall. A small Roman bridge, built in the Middle Ages, spans the Nive river. The house of St François-Xavier is situated by the "Porte de Navarre" which still has its original stone sentry boxes. Stairs lead to the rampart walk. The Sainte-Marie hospital for Compostela pilgrims was once adjacent to the bell tower.

Porte de Navarre

The Citadel

The Rue de la Citadelle

The Rue de la Citadelle is lined with beautiful facades of pink sandstone. On the door lintels you can read the history of certain families. This was the main street in the Middle Ages and it leads to the Porte de France. The Prison des évêques (the Bishops' prison) has several cells that housed many prisoners over the centuries, but never a Bishop though. The year 1584 is inscribed on the Bishops' house.
The Compostela pilgrims arrived through the Porte de St Jacques which is now listed as a world heritage site.
The Rue d'Espagne is lined with Navarre-style houses that have lintels stating the occupation of the inhabitants. The Maison des Etats de Navarre is very well preserved and saw its last assembly in 1789. The animal market takes place on the Place des Remparts. The citadel was restored in 1643 by Antoine Deville, after several disasters.
St Jean-pied-de-Port is still an important trading centre thanks to its fairs and markets.

◁ *The Notre-Dame-du-bout-du-pont church*

LES ALDUDES - ALDUDE

The Irouléguy vineyard

At the entrance of the Baigorry valley lies two beautiful villages, Les Aldudes and Urepel, surrounded by the Arlutxe and Harguibel Peaks and the Belaondo, Lastéguy and Mizpira cols.
The Haut Navarre-style houses are built of red sandstone. The church was built at the end of the 17th century and then altered in the 19th century. It holds the golden rosary that belonged to Maximilien, emperor of Mexico in the 19th century. The Esnazu chapel houses the altarpiece of the old Larressorre church.
The local economy depends on agriculture and breeding of sheep, cattle and the pink and black basque pigs that give a delicious ham.
There are three cromlechs at the Argibel site, a tomb made up of "menhirs" from the first millenium before our era. The "bordali" in the uplands is a small farm : the animals are kept on the groundfloor ; the hay on the first floor ; the shepherd lives further away in the "olha". The "cayolar" in the high mountains consists of a grazing area and an olha.

St Etienne de Baïgorry

Les Aldudes

The pink and black
basque pig

AROUND THE IRATY FOREST

The Laurhibar valley holds many protohistoric remains : cromlechs, dolmens, defense structures.
St James pilgrims passed through the village of St Jean-le-Vieux as early as the in 12th century. The Romanesque church porch dates back to the 12th century. A stone cross stands on the church square. A Roman camp was located here. The Château de Sant-Per was destroyed by Richard Lionheart in 1777. In Ahaxe only the ruins of the donjon and ramparts remain.
The Château Donamartia in Lecumberry dates back to the Middle Ages.

Iraty chalets

Behorléguy

The Behorléguy peak, a rocky spur, dominates the Arbailles forest and the village of Behorléguy with its remarkable church that holds several medieval statues. The 12th century Saint-Sauveur chapel is surrounded by a Way of the Cross with stone pillars. It holds a legendary candelabra that is said to be impossible to move.
The ascent towards Iraty and its magnificent forest is done via the Burdincurutcheta col (1100m).
A ridge road, south of St Jean-pied-de-port, leads to the Hostatéguy peak and to the Château-Pignon redoubt which was built in 1512. The Arnostéguy col is 1236 metres at its highest point and leads to the Urculu tower, the "Roman trophy".

La Soule

MAULEON-LICHARRE MAULE-LETXARRE

The fortified castle

Sandal manufacturing

The Gave du Saison, or Saison torrent, divides Mauléon in two. The lower part of the town is an industrial area where the espadrille manufacturers were regrouped. The Château d'Andurain is a renaissance castle built by Arnaud I, Bishop of Oloron in the 17th century.
The Hôtel de Montréal was built in the 17th century according to the plans of Mansart.
In the upper part of town stands the impressive 12th century fortified castle. Only the surrounding walls, three partly eroded towers and a prison remain.
The St Jean-de-Berraute chapel was built outside the town in the 11th century by the Knights of the Order of Malta. The hospital has disappeared but the St Jean chancel still stands in the middle of the cemetery.

Le Saison

The fronton

L'HOPITAL-SAINT-BLAISE - OSPITALE PIA

The village lies in the heart of a narrow wooded valley, formerly called l'Hôpital de la Miséricorde. It is settled on a secondary route to Santiago de Compostela and is now listed as a world heritage site by Unesco. The commander's residence has disappeared. The 12th century Hispano-Moorish style church was built in the shape of a Greek cross. It is topped by an octagonal lantern ; at the crossing of the transept is a ribbed dome supported by eight arches taking the shape of an eight-pointed star, a copy of a dome in the Great Mosque in Cordoba.
The chancel window openings are made up of stone slabs pierced with different motifs. During three days in February the church comes to life thanks to a pilgrimage in which only men participate.

TARDETS-SORHOLUS – ATHARRATZE-SORHOLÜZE

This is a fortified village founded in the 13th century. 17th century houses with archways surround its square.
Tardets and Sorholus were united in 1859.
The church is situated in Sorholus.
The houses that line the Saison have beautiful wood balconies on their back facades.
From the viewpoint at La Madeleine you can enjoy breathtaking views of the Peaks du Midi d'Ossau and Bigorre. Pilgrims come to the Madeleine chapel, which is built on a primitive place of worship.
The Tardets dancers are among the most renowned in the Soule province.

The Madeleine chapel

Le Saison

SAINTE-ENGRACE - SANTA-GRAZI

A narrow, winding road leads to this village, which is one of the most beautiful villages in Soule. It belonged to the San Salvador de Leyre monastery in Spain from the 11th to the 18th century and it was stopping place on the route to Compostela.
Its collegiate church was built in the second half of the 12th century. Inside it has polychrome sculptured stone capitals and a pulpit made of polychrome wood. An altarpiece describes the life of Sainte Engrace, a 3rd century martyr. The cemetery has very old disc-shaped steles.
The Ehujarre gorges, up to 500 metres deep, are very spectacular.

The Romanesque church

Capital with medieval decorations

The Ehujarre gorges

GORGES DE KAKOUETTA - KAKOETAKO ARROILA

The Kakouetta gorges stretch over 3500 metres. The walk starts at the bottom of the canyon and parts of it go over footbridges running along the cliff walls. The path leads around a lake and over a bridge before it follows two cliff faces that rise 300 metres up to the Benta resurgence, from where a waterfall flows out. Further along is the "Grotte du Lac". A cave with impressive stalactites and stalagmites.

Le grand étroit

The waterfall

LARRAU - LARRANE

Larrau was originally a priory and a hospital depending on the Abbey of Sauvelade.
This village, typical for the Soule province, is arranged around the church. The houses have pointed slate roofs.
The church was restored in 1655 and has a Romanesque apse. The St Joseph chapel, built by monks, is a place of pilgrimage. It was restored in 1861.
The road that follows the Orhy Peak offers a fantastic view all the way to the Erroymendi col, where people hunt ring doves.
An inn at the lieu-dit Logibar serves as point of departure for the walk to the Holçarte gorges. After about one hour the path leads over an impressive footbridge that overhangs the 150 metre deep Ohaldubi canyon.

The Holçarte footbridge

The Pixta waterfall

Guipuzcoa

IRUN

Irun is the most important industrial and commercial town in the Bidasoa region.
The Palacio de Arbelaiz in the Calle de la Iglesia where many famous personalities stayed over the centuries, was burnt down during the Spanish civil war in 1936. The town hall, inaugurated in 1763, was built in a traditional style and has a porch with archways.
The construction of the Notre-Dame de Juncal church lasted a century and it was finally finished in 1606. It is built in dressed stone supported by solid buttresses. The 14th century Santa Elena Hermitage has been a place of worship for twenty centuries. Its museum houses the remains of a Roman temple and many archaeological vestiges. The Santa Elena fountain is situated in the vicinity.

The Renaissance-style Palacio de Urdanibia was built in 1612. The San Juan Harri monolith is a stone column with a shaft ending with a capital decorated with crowns. The San Martial chapel was built to commemorate a victory against the French in 1522. The chapel has been damaged several times. A mirador offers a fantastic panorama.

The San Martial's procession

Calle Mayor

FONTARRABIE - HONDARRIBIA

Cape Higuer that dominates Fuenterrabia offers a fantastic viewpoint.
Due to its location at the mouth of the Bidasoa the town was fortified as early as in the 12th century.
The fishermen's quarter is characterised by its typical colourful houses. The Santa Maria Magdalena church and the San Pedro cofradia are situated here.
The old quarter is surrounded by walls and entered through the Puerta de Santa Maria which bears the town's arms.
The Charles Quint's castle was originally built by the King of Navarra in 980. Today it is a parador but it once served as fortress and residence for kings and governors. It was partly destroyed by the French in 1794.
A large number of 18th century houses line the main street.
The Gothic-style Nuestra Señora de l'Asuncion y del Manzano church stood finished in 1549 ; it has magnificent Gothic crenelles and altarpieces dedicated to San Antonio and San Miguel.

Frontage

The remparts

The castle of San Telmo was built in 1598 in order to protect the Asturiaga port and the entrance of the estuary.
On the road leading to the peak of the Jaizkibel lies the Sanctuary of Nuestra Señora de Guadalupe, named after the town's patron saint. This Gothic-style sanctuary was probably built in the 16th century.
A procession of silence goes through the streets of the town on Good Friday.
Atun eguna, tuna day, and Sardina eguna, sardine day, are held in August.

Txingudi's bay

The old quarter

Santa Maria church

PASAJES - PASAIA

After following the ridge of the Jaizkibel one looks down on the port of Pasajes that is built in three districts around a small river.
In Pasajes de San Juan "Pasaia Donibane" you can admire a large altarpiece in the San Juan Bautista church and discover the simple fishermen's houses with colourful balconies and arched galleries built on the edge of the cliff. The Villaviciosa palace where Victor Hugo lived for a time is situated here. The Marquis de La Fayette chose this port to embark for America.
A shuttle goes over to the other bank.
Pasajes de San Pedro "Pasai San Pedro" is another fishing village.
The more industrial Pasajes Ancho "Pasai Antxo" is the port of San Sebastian.

The square

The port entrance

SAINT-SEBASTIEN – DONOSTIA

Originally the city of San Sebastian consisted of a fishing port built against a fortified village and an agricultural enclave. The rest of it was only marshland.
Between the 13th and 19th centuries twelve fires partly destroyed the city. The last one, in August 1813, completely ruined it. Queen Isabel II who, on her doctor's advice, took seawater baths in the city allowed for the demolition of the ramparts in the old quarters and the construction of the new town in 1863.
The old town, at the feet of Monte Urgull, is typical of the region with its port and quay with small houses, its old, lively streets lined with restaurants and "pintxos", bars.
Donostia and its surroundings are a gastronomic wonderland : enjoy txangurro (crab) filled with its own meat, elvers (piballes) and other seafoods.
The peculiarity of the Plaza de la Constitucion are the

The Plaza de la Constitucion

The bay of San Sebastian

houses with numbered balconies ; this square used to be an arena.
The Santa Maria del Coro basilica has a magnificent Baroque portal and twin towers.
You get to the port through the Quay gate "Portaletas". The Aquarium and the Museo Naval are situated at the end of the quay.
On the peak of Monte Urgull stand the remains of the Santa Cruz de la Mota castle and the Cristo de la Mota chapel ; this site has a network of paths leading to the Sagrado Corazon, Sacred Heart.
Donostia is a very nice city criss-crossed by wide streets lined with opulent buildings and beautiful hotels. Across from the town hall are beautiful gardens and La Concha with its fine sandy beach.
In this fantastic bay lies the Isla de Santa Clara, and at its southern end rises the Monte Igueldo which you can get to by road or with the funicular to enjoy the view of the bay, the coast and the mountains.
On the Plaza de Guipuzcoa with its garden and ponds stands the monumental building of the Diputacion.

Tapas bar

Santa Maria del Coro basilica

The Kursaal

The harbour

LATA FRIA
0,50
Coca-Cola

La Concha beach and the town hall

The cathedral

The 19th century Buen Pastor cathedral in Neo-Classic style is situated in Calle Loyola.

Several bridges span the “Urumea” river ; the bridge closest to the rivermouth leads to the Zurriola beach and the futuristic Kursaal convention centre.

The Maria-Christina bridge is the most monumental of all the bridges.

Several cinema and jazz festivals are held every year ; the tamborrada, parade with around sixty parties of drummers ; a trainerillas run, competition for traditional fishing boats.

Apart from the Aquarium and the Museo Naval you can also visit ; the Museo Diocesano with religious art from between the 13th and 20th centuries ; the Museo Cemento Rezola dedicated to the history of concrete and the Museo de San Telmo, an old Dominican convent that houses archaeological and ethnographical exhibitions, an art collection as well as an exhibition dedicated to the marine world, and ; the Miramon Kutxa science museum.

LOYOLA - LOIOLA

The Sanctuary of Loyola stands not far from Azpeitia. The site was built in the 17th and 18th centuries around the Loyola house, in honour of St Ignatius of Loyola, who was born in 1491 into a powerful Basque noble family.

Alter 30 years serving the court and the army in Castile and Navarre, Ignatius was convalescing from wounds suffered during the defence of Pamplona in 1521 when he found God and left to lead the life of a hermit for a year.

For thirteen years following this, he travelled the world as a pilgrim of God.

In 1523 he visited Jerusalem, after which he attended the universities of Alcalá, Salamanca and Paris.

In 1537, he was ordained as a priest in Venice.

He died in Rome on 31 July 1556, leaving behind him his apostolic work as a legacy.

The sanctuary was built by the Basque masters Zaldua, Lecuna and Ignacio de Ibero. Its most outstanding feature is the baroque basilica, crowned by a great dome designed by the Italian architect Carlo Fontana.

The basilica

The basilica also houses a magnificent organ.

One wing of the building, on the banks of the River Urola, houses a museum and audiovisual exhibition devoted to the work of St Ignatius of Loyola.

The dome

The sanctuary

OÑATE - OÑATI

Oñate, perhaps Basque town that has best conserved its traditional character, is also famed as one of the most monumental sites in Guipúzcoa.
The town lies in a valley in the southwest of the province, nestling beside the mountains and watched over by Mount Aloña.
Oñate did not become part of Guipúzcoa until 1845. The local people are considered to be brave, hardy folk, proud to remind all and sundry that the conquistador Aguirre was from these lands.
Between the 14th and 18th centuries, two great families, the Garibays and the Uribarris, were constantly feuding as they vied for control of the region. Finally, in the 18th century, the two families came together to jointly mine the iron that was found here in abundance.
The University of Santi-Spiritus, founded in 1540 by Don Rodrigo, a friend of Cardinal Cisneros, is the repository of historic archives comprising more than 12,000 volumes.
The Church of San Miguel, a Gothic monument dating back to the 15th century, houses a splendid Flamboyant Gothic cloister.
The most outstanding attractions in Oñate include the old town with the Plaza de los Fueros (a partially fortified square), the baroque Town Hall and many palaces and noble mansions.

The university Santi-Spiritus

The sanctuary

ARANTZAZU – ARANZAZU

The sanctuary of Arantzazu stands amidst magnificent natural scenery, embellished even more by the outstanding beauty of the mountains along the route to the three churches situated in the towns of Azpeitia, Zumárraga and Oñate. According to legend, in 1468 a shepherd called Rodrigo de Balzategi discovered an image of Our Lady amongst some thorns whilst he watched over his flock of goats. This was considered a miracle, and Our Lady of Arantzazu was venerated for centuries and made the patron saint of Guipúzcoa.
A chapel was built here, but was destroyed more than once in wars and by fire. The sanctuary was rebuilt in 1950, flanked by three limestone towers, in work carried out by the architects Sainz de Oiza and Louis de Laorga. The figures on the façade are by the sculptor Jorge Oteiza. The steep staircase leads up to the basilica doors, which were designed by Eduardo Chillida. The nave is adorned by an altarpiece made from 600 m2 of carved wood and painted al fresco by Lucio Munos. Installed in the crypt is a painting of Christ Resuscitated by Néstor Basterretxea. Celebrations in honour of Our Lady of Arantzazu are held on September 9 each year. Moreover, pilgrimages to the sanctuary from towns and villages in the surrounding provinces take place from May to October.

The sanctuary

The nave

The fresco

THE GUIPUZCOA'S COAST

This coastline is exceptional : seaside towns and villages, hills and meadows, cliffs, rivermouths with fishing ports appearing around the bend of a winding road.

Zarautz is one of the most beautiful beaches on the coast ; it is a very popular holiday resort. Here you can discover the Palacio de Narros, the Luzea tower, the Palacio de Portu and the Nuestra Señora la Real church. The Museo Escuela del Mar "Itxas natura" houses six aquariums and a museum dedicated to photography.

The beach of Zarautz

The torre Luzea

Getaria, a bustling typical Guipuzcoa fishing village. The couturier Balenciaga was born here and his foundation is open for visits. The Gothic-style San Salvador church was built in the 15th century ; the Monte San Anton with its mouse-shaped silhouette stands out against the sea. The numerous restaurants in the village serve "chipirones pelayo" based on fresh squid and confit onions.

The port of Getaria

The San Salvador church and the Monte San Anton

Zumaia

The towns of **Deba** and **Zumaia** were holiday resorts for wealthy families from Bilbao and its surroundings. Zumaia offers the two beaches Itzurun and Santiago but also the museum of the painter Zuloaga which is situated in a garden on the seafront and has a chapel, a cloister and a studio.
The Santiago chapel was a stopping place on St James's way.
The San Telmo hermitage sits on the cliff that overhangs the harbour.

Deba

The Basque Gothic-style San Pedro church is a fortified construction from the 16th century.
Itzurun beach is dominated by pink and grey cliffs.

The Gothic-style Asuncion church in Deba has been declared a national monument ; admire its magnificent polychrome stone portal and its Arabian-inspired cloister.

Mutriku

Mutriku is another beautiful fishing port where you can savour mackerels prepared according to various recepies. The Berdel eguna, mackerel day, is held here on the first Saturday in April. Inland specialities are hake with clams and barbs and green peppers stuffed with veal tail.
The village is built on a cliff and overlooks the port and its lively, sloping alleys. Discover the Zabiel palace in the street leading to the Plaza Txurruka with its Neo-Classic style church.

Viscaya

ONDARROA

The port and the beach

The Santa Maria church by the canal

The beautiful winding coast continues with coves and bays.

Ondarroa is a large fishing port situated by the mouth of Rio Artibai. It is specialised in industrial fishing and has several canning factories. The Gothic Santa Maria church was built in the 15th century and the Nuestra Señora de la Antigua church in the 16th century. The Puento Viejo links the banks of the river and another bridge, Puente de Hierro is situated by the mouth of the Artibai. In Ondarroa you can enjoy txirlas, small clams with garlic and onions, as well as sea bream and stuffed squid served in its own ink.

LEKEITIO

Lekeitio is a seaside resort with fine sandy beaches. In front of the small fishing port are plenty of restaurants and bars with terraces. The Santa Maria de la Asuncion church on the Plaza de los Fueros was built in the 16th century and holds a Flemish altarpiece. Several palaces, as well as a Dominican convent founded in the 14th century line the narrow streets. The 17th century San Juan hermitage is situated close to the jetty. The pine covered island of San Nicolaus lies right in front of the beach. The Feria de San Antolin, with watergames in the port, is held at the beginning of September.

The road, leaving Lekeitio, is lined with eucalyptus and goes down into the land between meadows and basque farms. Elantxobe is a lovely little village with paved alleys and a colourful fishing port, situated in the centre of a bay.
The Santimamine caves, magnificent natural caves with animal paintings, are situated in Kortezubi.

The beach of Karraspio

The port and the church Santa Maria de la Asuncion

GUERNIKA-LUMO

The square

The estuary of the Urdaibai river has been declared a natural biosphere reserve by Unesco. The reason for this is the constant inflow of salt water at the bottom of the valley which mixes with the fresh water from the rivers. The valley is completely dry at low tide.

The town Guernika on the Rio Oka was unfortunately made famous by the German airforce bombing in 1937. You can visit the Casa de Juntas, the Assembly house or Parliament of Bizkaia, which was spared by the bombs ; the Museo de Euskal Herria, the Guernika Museo and the Parque de los pueblos de Europa, a park with works of Chillida and Henry Moore. The remains of the oak of Guernika, a sacred tree for the Basque people, can be seen in a mausoleum. Another oak was planted and assemblies are held under it. The culinary speciality of the town is fried small green peppers "gernikako piperrak".

The oak of Guernika

MUNDAKA

The town of Mundaka, further up the estuary, is famous for its beach and its "spot" that attracts surfers from all over the world. From its hills yo can enjoy the most beautiful panoramic view of the Biscaya.
The village is very welcoming with plenty of small squares shaded by plane trees, narrow alleys and colourful boats along the quays.
The rocky island of Izaro with its abandoned Franciscan convent is situated right in front of Mundaka.

The harbour

The Santa Catalina hermitage

The harbour entrance

BERMEO

The harbour, the Santa Maria and Santa Eufemia churches

Fishing boats

Bermeo, next to Mundaka, is one of the most important towns in the province and an important fishing port. The Museo del Pescador, dedicated to fishing, is set up in the Ercilla tower. The Santa Eufemia church is built in Gothic style. Bermeo's restaurants serve plenty of different kinds of fish : hake, sea bream, salt cod, squid and the marmitako, tuna and potatoe ragout with tomatoes, peppers and onions.

On the day of San Roch people bring their picnic baskets to the Atalaya park to celebrate a feast.

THE ISLAND OF SAN-JUAN DE GAZTELUGATXE

The peninsula

The hermitage

The island of San-Juan de Gaztelugatxe is connected to the mainland via a stonebridge ; 232 steps lead to the top of the island, its Way of the Cross is lined with 14 stations. The Romanesque-style building belonged to Templar monks. The interior of the hermitage is dedicated to seamen and it holds the prow of a ship and has a propeller embedded in one wall. The annual processions held on 24 June, 31 July and 29 August, attract large crowds.
A monastery and a hospice for pilgrims were built here in 1053 ; they were both destroyed at the end of the 16th century by pirates during a French-English expedition.
The entire Bay of Viscaya as well as the Machichaco lighthouse can be seen from this fantastic viewpoint.

BILBAO - BILBO

Bilbao is the capital of Biscaya, the financial and economic centre of the Basque Country and a large fishing port.
It was founded in the Middle-Ages and built on both banks of the Nervion river.
The agriculture disappeared little by little leaving room for seamen and smiths.
The province has exploited its iron deposits since Roman times and this has resulted in a heavy iron and steel industry. Bilbao was an important port for goods shipped all over Europe and to America as early as in the 16th century. Internationally renowned events take place several times a year in the Exhibition centre.
Since the construction of the Museo Guggenheim in 1997, Bilbao has been transformed into a modern cosmopolitan city. This original building made of glass, stone, steel and titanium is the work of the architect Frank O. Gehry. Its 11000 m^2 are entirely dedicated to contemporary and modern art.
The Palacio Euskalduna, a convention and music centre is situated on the site of the old shipyards.

The harbour

The Bizkaia suspension bridge

The town hall and the Rio Nervion

During its transformation the city of Bilbao built an underground.

The Muelle de la Merced is an old convent that has been converted into a municipal music and theatre centre. The old town has kept its charm ; it was restored following serious floods in 1983. Along its many pedestrian streets you can discover modern and traditional shops, tapas bars, called "pintxos" in the Basque Country, and plenty of gastronomic and traditional restaurants serving for exemple sardines, salt cod and spinach tarts.

The San Anton church is built in a combination of Gothic and Renaissance styles. The San Anton bridge as well as the Ribera market date back to 1878.

The Gothic Santiago cathedral was built at the end of the 14th century. Don't miss the Portal del Angel and the Plaza Nueva where the Sunday market and the "Feria de San Tomas" are held. There are plenty of bars under the arcades in the Plaza. The Arriaga theatre with its sumptuous interior is situated on the Paseo del Arenal, a promenade along the "ria". On the other bank you can discover the Baroque-style church of

Euskalduna bridge and Rio Nervion

The Gran via and Plaza Moyúa

Getxo

The old town

The Doña Casilda de Iturriza park

Frontage

San Vicente church

The beach of Sopelana

Arenal bridge

San Nicolas with its twin towers, the town hall and the University of Deusto run by the Society of Jesus. The busy Puente del Arenal links the old town to Ensanche, the new district.
The Gran via runs from the Plaza de España or Cicular, where the statue of the city's founder Don Diego Lopez de Haro stands, to the Plaza del Sagrado Corazon with a stone column crowned with a bronze statue of the "Sagrado Corazon", the Sacred Heart. This is the main financial and commercial street of the capital where the big shops, the banks and several important buildings are situated : "La Diputacion Foral de Bizkaia", regional council of Biscaya, "la Hacienda Estatal", the state tax office, the "Gobierno Civil", the police headquarters, and the Carlton hotel.
The San Vicente church and the Albia gardens with its famous Café Iruña are situated close to the Gran Via. The Doña Casilda de Iturrizar park is the largest green area in the city : gardens, paths, pergolas and a duck pond makes it a lovely area to take a walk in.
The Fine Arts museum holds important collections from various schools.
The "El Arenal" garden is a large, much-frequented public garden offering different activities.
A funicular goes from the Old town up to Artxanda from where you can overlook the city and admire the Nuestra Señora de Begoña Basilic.
Other than the Guggenheim and the Fine Arts museum you can also visit the Museo de Pasos de Semana Santa, relating to the Holy Week, the Museo Taurino dedicated to the history of bullfighting, the Museo Montren, a museum of trains from the 1920's to our time, the Museo Diocesano de Arte Sacro and the Museo Arqueologico.

General view of the city

The Guggenheim museum

Alava

VITORIA-GASTEIZ

The Plaza de la Virgen Blanca

Vitoria, capital of Alava and the independant Basque community, is famous for its hospitality. It has a strategic position at the crossing of several roads and it is surrounded by mountains, lakes, plains and vineyards producing the famous Rioja Alavesa wine.
The Alava is famous for its market gardening that supplies the entire province and several other regions with different vegetables : artichokes, cardoons, French beans, courgettes, beetroot, peas, aubergines, lettuce, cabbage, leek and broad beens. Vitoria has plenty of good restaurants and a cooking competition with potatoe-based recepies is organised every year. The province has kept the tradition of producing brandies, particularly the patxaran that is very appreciated in the Basque Country.
The old town in Vitoria that was declared historic monument in 1997, has kept its medieval charm : narrow, pedestrian streets, houses with coats of arms, Renaissance palaces and Gothic churches. The church of San Miguel where the patron saint of the city “la Virgen Blanca”, is worshipped, is situated on the Plaza de la Virgen Blanca. A monument dedicated to the battle of Vitoria also stands here. Don’t miss the Renaissance-style Palacio de los Alava Esquibel ; the Gothic San Pedro church ; the old customs building ; the Urbina Zarate palace and the Dona Otxanda tower that holds the Natural science museum. On the Plaza Santo Domingo stands the Fuente de los Patos, the duck fountain, and the Velasco-Berastegui palace. The Gobeo Guevara San Juan palace, that now holds the museum of archeology, and the beautiful brick construction “El Portalon” are situated in Calle Correira. During the visit you can also discover the Torre de los Hurtado de Anda, the palace of the Marquis del Fresno, the Gothic-style Santa-Maria cathedral built in the 13th and 14th centuries, the Escoriaza Esquibel palace, the Montehermoso palace that houses a cultural centre, the San Vicente church and the remains of the old town walls.

A mirador offers a view of a large part of the city. The Villasuso or Martin de Salinas palace stands next to the San Bartolome steps and the Plaza del Machete. Continuing under “los Arquillos”, the arcades, to the San Fransisco slope we come to the Casa del Cordon and the Bendana palace which houses the Fournier de Naipes museum that holds over 18000 deck of cards of all sorts and ages. The Santa Cruz convent and the old hospice are situated in the Calle San Vicente de Paul. Most of these medieval buildings are now museums or cultural centres. A large number of craft workshops and restaurants make this old town a very lively place. Next to the San Miguel church is “los Arquillos”, a construction with stairs and porticos linking the old and the new districts via the Plaza de España with the town hall. The sculptor Chillida designed the Plaza de Fueros. The San Antonio convent is situated on the Plaza General Loma.
In the magnificent Florida park starts a 3 km walk along which you can discover the Basque Parliament, the Neo-Gothic style Nueva cathedral, the Provincia palace, head office of the Diputación Foral de Alava, the Regional council.
Its lovely walks make Vitoria even more beautiful : the Sentier walk on which the Zulueta palace is situated,

The San Miguel church

La Casa del Portalon in the medieval quarter

and the Armentia walk with the beautiful Romanesque San Prudencio basilica, the Fray Francisco walk with the Army museum as well as the Fine Arts museum, the Prado park, the Judimendi park built on the site of an old Jewish cemetery, the Juan de Arriaga park with a lake surrounded by an amphitheatre, and the San Juan chapel. The many parks also contributes to the city’s beauty.
Vitoria is a very nice city that has known a late urban development. It has many parks, gardens, wide avenues and pedestrian streets and it is a city that has kept its traditions intact. But it is also a financial, cultural and sport centre with two convention centres and it has an efficient transport system thanks to its airport, its motorways and its bus station.

ANANA

The village and the salt marshes

The Santa Maria de Villcones church

An incredible scenery suddenly appears out of a wasteland : the Añana salt marshes. A 17° water saturated with salt runs from the Fuentelmuera spring since Roman times. It was canalised thanks to a rudimentary system of wood gutters on piles. From May to September all these terraces or "eras", made up a fantastic landscape of white salt. There were up to 5000 "eras". Today there are still 300 eras in use and they supply the ham salting rooms.
A few houses with elaborate balconies and the 13th century Santa-Maria de Villacones church witness of the town's rich past.
The convent of the order of San Juan de Acre dominates the village.

Navarra

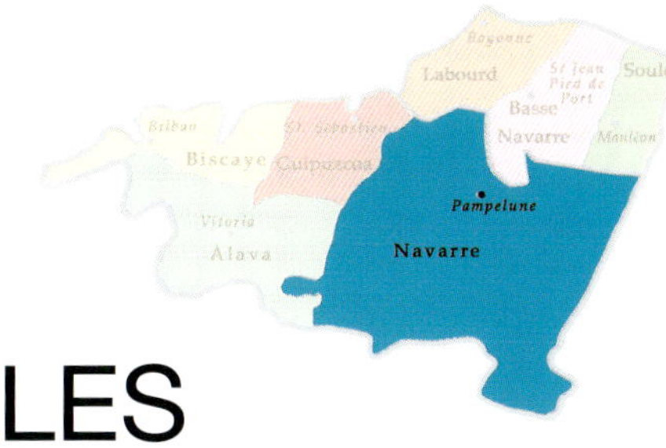

RONCEVAUX - RONCESVALLES

The most mythical road in the Pyrenees goes from St Jean Pied de Port, then through the villages Arneguy and Valcarlos right up to the Ibaneta col between steep cliffs before it reaches Roncesvalles.
It is situated on the most important route to Santiago de Compostela and plenty of pilgrims passed through the village already in the Middle Ages. The monastery is an impressive building with a zink roof.
The Gothic-style collegiate church was built in the 13th century. It has a Virgin statue made of cedar wood decorated with gold and precious stones.
The cloister which was destroyed by snow masses in 1600 was rebuilt in a severe style. It contains the San Augustan chapel where the King of Navarra Sancho the Strong and his wife are buried. The Las Navas de Tolosa chains are laid by their feet.

The church

Coaching inn

The monastery

PAMPELUNE – IRUNA

Pamplona's origins go back to the year 75 BC. The city's population grew rapidly ; 29000 inhabitants in 1900, 72000 in 1950 and close to 200000 today. Several quarters were built during the 20th century to face the population increase. The university of Navarra was founded and an industrial centre was built as well as hotels, hospitals and facilities for sports and culture.

The Sarasate promenade links the new and old town. Here you can discover the old Law courts ; the Lois de Navarra monument "Monumento à los Fueros de Navarra" and the San-Nicolas church. The castle square, "Plaza del Castillo" is considered the heart of Pamplona. It was the parade ground of the first castle and tournaments and bullfights were held here from 1651. A fountain was built in 1788 and then a pavilion. The bullfights were organised here until 1844. The square is surrounded by arcades and 18th century buildings. It is a very lively place with its many bars with terraces, of which one is the "Café Iruña" made famous by Hemingway.

The Neo-Classic Diputacion Foral palace which is the office of the Regional council of Navarra is situated on Avenida de Carlos III. The recently restored cathedral has a Gothic-style interior with three aisles and an ambulatory. It holds a silver statue of Santa-Maria la Real, a choir with a Gothic gate of wrought iron and a number of remarkable altarpieces. The alabaster tomb of Carlos III the Noble and his wife Dona Leonor de Trastamara is also found in here. The Gothic-style cloister has several magnificent doors like that of the Virgin of Amparo and the Preciosa, and it houses Gothic sepulchres and the chapel of Bishop Barbazan with a star-shaped vault. You can visit the Diocesan museum and see its collection of Roman, Gothic, Renaissance and Baroque sculptures as well as paintings and works of gold- and silver dating from the 12th to the 19th century.

The Redin bastion with its "gate to France", or Zumalacarregui gate ; the Rampart walk ; the Plaza Santa Maria la Real with the Archiepiscopal

The San Lorenzo church

Plaza del Castillo

The town hall

San Saturnino church

Shop

palace can be reached from the San Joseph square. The town hall and the Navarra museum have beautiful Baroque facades. The museum holds a fantastic collection of mosaics, Gothic wall paintings, a Hispano-Arabian ivory casket as well as a painting of San Adrian de Goya. A Baroque chapel of the Virgin of the Saint James path is built in the old cloister of the San Saturnin or San Cernin church.
The Audit office is the only Baroque civil building in Pamplona. The "La Agricola" building, office of the library of the Independant community, is situated on the Plaza de San Francisco.
On the small Plaza del Consejo stands a fountain and the Guendulain palace. The Baroque facade of the Ezpeleta palace and the San Lorenzo church with the San Fermin chapel and the square of the Convent of the Recollets, can be seen in the Calle Mayor. The Taconera park is a romantic park with wide alleys and charming nooks. It is a fantastic botanical garden with peacocks, deer, ducks and swans. The old San Nicolas gate stands here.
The citadel, started in 1571, was a pentagonal fortification with five arrowhead-shaped bastions in the angles. It is nice to take a walk in its surrounding gardens "la Vuelta del Castillo".
Several other parks surround the city in the new town : the Halfmoon park, the Biurdana park, the Vaguada, the gardens of the University of Navarra, the Yamaguchi park.
Pamplona is worldfamous thanks to its San Fermin feria held at the beginning of July every year ; people run in front of loose bulls in the city streets, from Corral to the arenas, every morning at 8h. The feria in Pamplona goes on for 9 days and offers traditional and cultural activities. The fireworks open the feria, the vespers are sung in the San Fermin chapel, there are processions, brass bands, bagpipers, a parade of giants, bull running and bandas.
All participants are dressed in white with red scarves and belts.

Santa Maria cathedral

The ramparts

San Fermin

PUENTE LA REINA

The bridge on the Arga

The Crucifijo church

The two main pilgrim routes to Santiago de Compostela join in Puente la Reina.
The bridge on the Arga was built on order by a Queen of Navarra in the 11th century and it gave the village its name ("The Queen's bridge). The village was developed thanks to the large number of pilgrims travelling through.
The 12th century Crucifijo church was adjacent to the hospice, where the pilgrims arrived ; only the portal with its animals and mythical monsters is original. The church holds a magnificent Christ statue of wood and a polychrome Virgin with Child from the 12th century.
The 14th century Santiago church has kept its original portal. The six-arched Roman bridge from the 14th century was the point of departure for the Compostela pilgrims.
The Calle Mayor is lined with houses with coats of arms and wrought iron balconies.

ESTELLA - LIZARRA

Estella was an important stopping place on the route to Santiago de Compostela and the village has many monuments. The oldest part of the village is situated south of the river. The Franks settled here and from the Middle Ages this is where the most beautiful houses, inns, hospices as well as the San Pedro de la Rua church with its impressive tower, 13th century Romanesque portal and its cloister, were found.
The Calle de la Rua, the old main street, is lined with Gothic and Renaissance-style houses. The Santo Sepulcro church shows a French influence with a finely sculptured portal and a Gothic facade.
The Romanesque-style Kings of Navarra palace built in the 12th century is situated on the Plaza San Martin.
A Jewish community settled in the east of the village, in the Juderia quarter.
Another quarter was built around the San Miguel church ; its Northern portal is Romanesque-influenced and it has a Gothic interior and a Baroque altarpiece. This is a commercial quarter.

The San Juan Bautista church is situated on the Plaza de Los Fueros.
Calle Mayor is known for its beautiful houses.

San Miguel quarter

San Pedro cloister

ARTAJONA

The fortified San Saturnino church

Artajona is a medieval fortified enclave with twelve donjons and surrounding walls built in the 11th century. The fortress-church of San Saturnino was built in the 13th century on top of the ruins of a Romanesque temple. It preserves a parapet walk and its facade has a sculptured Gothic tympanum.
The Square tower holds a 16th century altarpiece, a black Gothic Virgin and a shrine.
A hermitage at the end of the village houses the Virgin of Jerusalem, a work of metal brought back from the Crusades.

A sculptured Gothic tympanum

SANGÜESA - ZANGOZA

The bridge and the Santa Maria la Real church

The door of the Santa Maria church

This town was originally built on the Rocaforte rock to protect Pamplona from Muslim invasions. In the 12th century the King Alfonso I founded a new town on the plain.

Numerous pilgrims on their way to Santiago de Compostela stopped here and stayed in the town's many inns, hospices and palaces. The town got richer. The King decided to have a palace built here and the knights of San Juan set up a commander's residence. A Jewish community settled here.

Sanguesa enjoyed royal privileges ; its pre-Renaissance cultural and architectural heritage is substantial, but when the pilgrimage declined Sanguesa fell into oblivion.

The portal of the 12th century Santa Maria la Real church is a masterpiece of Spanish-Romanesque style with numerous medieval sculptures. Discover the immense 16th century altarpiece and the dome overhanging the transept inside the church.

The Palace of the Prince of Viana with its Renaissance facade, crenellated towers, and inner ditch now houses the town hall.

CASTILLO DE JAVIER

As a recognition of their loyal services the ancestors of Francisco de Javier were given this 10th century fortress by the Count of Champagne. In 1512 the Castilla invaded Navarra. All the fortresses were demolished and the land was confiscated. The walls and towers of the seigneurial residence were razed to the ground. The future San-Francisco-Javier went to Paris to study theology.

Of the castle only the crenellated polygonal enclosure and the Christo tower remain.
The Palacio Nuevo and the Santa Maria church were built in the 16th century. The church houses a 14th century Risen Christ, a Romanesque 13th century Virgin and a wall painting representing The Dance of Death.
The castle has been undergoing restoration since 1950 and is now a museum.

LEYRE - YESA

LEYRE MONASTERY

Leyre monastery is situated in a strategic position in wonderful surroundings. It became one of the main stopping places on the route to Santiago de Compostela at the end of the 9th century. The monastery was consecrated in 1057 and fell into oblivion in the 19th century. The Benedictine monks of Santo Domingo de Silos settled here in 1954. They dedicate themselves to Gregorian singing and liturgical studies.
This edifice consists of several buildings. The apse of the Romanesque church dates back to the 11th century. The crypt is the oldest part of the monastery. The Gothic style Upper church was built in the 14th century and it holds the tomb of the Kings of Navarra. It has a Romanesque-style chancel and a large 12th century western portal that was installed after the construction of the nave. The monastery buildings and the Palace of the Kings of Navarra were built in the 17th century in Aragonian style. A Hospederia, country inn, has been created in these buildings.

Leyre monastery

Yesa lake

YESA LAKE

The construction of a dam in the middle of the 20th century made the rocky landscape of the Sierra de Leyre less arid and allowed for the creation of the 14 kilometre long Yesa lake.
Numerous canals irrigate the dried soil all the way to the north of Bardenas Reales and Cinco Villas.

OLITE

The Middle Ages are present in all the alleys in old Olite ; in its stairs, stalls, nooks, its ramparts and many noble houses with coats of arms and balconies.
El Palacio de los Reyes de Navarra is a wonderful castle built in the 15th century by King Carlos III the Noble.
French and Spanish architects and artists contributed to its construction. The French influence is found in its towers and fireplaces. It was a castle with a sumptious interior : polychrome glass windows, gilded roofs, sculptured ceilings, a multitude of earthenware tiles on the walls and floor, hanging gardens, aviaries, a dovecote as well as an egg-shaped room where the ice was kept.
The castle was left in decline for many years and then partly damaged by a fire in 1813. It has recently been restored.
The Santa Maria la Real church, that once was the Royal chapel, has a magnificently sculptured 14th century portal. It houses a wonderful 16th century altarpiece and a 13th century Christ on the cross.
The San Pedro Apostol church with its Gothic tower has beautiful religious objects and a large altarpiece. Its cloister was built in Romanesque style.
The San Francisco monastery is said to have been founded by San Francisco himself. The Virgen del Colera, patron saint of Olite is worshipped here.
The 18th century Santa Engracia monastery was first transformed into a hospital of the San-Antonio order before it became a Clarisse convent.
Under the Carlos III square are two medieval galleries. Some parts of Roman and Medieval walls still remain.

Santa Maria la Real church

The Royal palace

TUDELA

The bridge on the Ebre (380 m)

Tudela, the second largest city in Navarra, was for a long time Pamplona's rival city.
The city was founded by the Arabs in 802 and conquered by the Normans on behalf of the King of Navarra in 1119.
Muslims, Jews and Arabs lived together on good terms for 400 years and this created a great cultural and architectural development.
The Jews were thrown out of the city at the end of the 15th century and the non-Christianized Muslims soon after that. This led to the decline of the city, but it was later to become an important market gardening centre. The Muslim-style bridge that spans the Erbe is 380 metres long, has 17 arches and once had defence towers.
The Romano-Gothic style cathedral was built on the ruins of a mosque in the 12th and 13th centuries. It houses several richly decorated chapels and a cloister with capitals bearing sculptures representing the life of Christ. The cathedral's beautiful portal represents the Last Judgement.
The Romanesque-style San Nicolas church was altered in the 18th century ; only the 12th century portal is original.
One of the oldest vestiges in the city is the Moorish-style Monreal tower.

Only the ruins remain of Sancho the Strong's castle. The 12th century Santa Magdalena church was built on the site of a Mozarab church.
You can discover the Palace of the Marquis de San Adrian with sculptures on its porch roof and the Santa Maria church, both built in Renaissance-style.
There are several Baroque-style buildings in Tudela ; the Plaza de los Fueros with its pavilion lined with houses with wrought iron balconies, the San Jorge church, the Dominican church and the Palace of the Marquis de Huarte.
Tudela is situated in the Ribera valley and it benefits from a micro-climate favourable for fruit and vegetable growing.

Cathedral, the Portal of Judgement

General view

THE BARDENAS REALES

To the south of Navarra lies a vast desert area, the Bardenas Reales, that is divided into three zones : El Plano in the north ; La Blanca in the centre and La Negra in the south.
This area was originally a mountain chain that gradually disappeared and was replaced by a marine gulf. This gulf was slowly filled up with sediments due to the erosion and it disappeared thousands of years ago. Today only salt deposits remain.
The main part of Bardenas was once covered with forests but they were overexploited up until the 19th century.
Rains are rare but violent here, which explains the soil erosion and gullying that with time create deep ravines. The Ciezo, a dry wind, increases the drought ; the temperatures can reach 40°C in the summer.
No people live in the Bardenas but it has served as a landmark for brigands over the centuries.

El Plano, a vast plateau with round hills, is the most welcoming of the zones. It is made up of farming fields where mainly cereal is grown. There is only one ravine here and at its widest point there is a pond, the El Ferial, inhabited by frogs, crayfish, tenches and ducks.
The Velado de Eguaras natural reserve is planted with pine, oak, juniper and rosemary. A part of the land is cultivated and inhabited by birds of prey, snakes, foxes, rabbits and wild boars. Every year flocks of sheep are moved to summer pastures in the lowlands of the Bardenas, along the same paths used for centuries, the "canadas".
La Blanca, situated at the centre of the Bardenas Reales, is the most arid area. La Blanca Baja is relatively flat with a few tabular hills and some fairy chimneys. It is made up of a clayey, jagged soil filled with cracks and sharp crests. The torrential rains dig out the hillsides leaving grey, white and yellow colours. Two ponds have been created in natural hollows. The higher La Blanca Alta is trenched by a large number of ravines.
La Negra consists of high plateaus : it is framed by the Valdenovillas ravine in the south and the Tudela ravine in the north. The rainwater carves deep ravines before flowing into the Ebre.
Las Caidas is a southern natural reserve with a vast pine forest. Other forests where pine and oak trees blend their dark colours have given La Negra its name. Wild boars, foxes, badgers, wildcats and owls can be found here.
The Rincon del Bu natural reserve is completely different : the vegetation is rare and poor ; the plain is arid with a few hills and tabular massifs with deeply gullied faces. There are foxes, hares and birds of prey living in this area.

FAUNA AND FLORA

The basque Country is situated on both sides of the Pyrenees and it has very different climates and a varied fauna and flora.
The three coastal provinces have a mild and humid temperate climate and a rich small mammal fauna. In the winter the vast humid areas, like the Urdaibai estuary, declared a natural biosphere reserve by Unesco, or the Txingudi bay receive plenty of migratory birds from Scandinavia. Ducks, spoonbills but also herons and sandpipers are amongst the most common migratory birds to come to these protected areas.
On higher altitudes the oak forests are replaced by beeches which is the dominating species of trees in the mountains. The Iraty forest is considered the largest beech forest in Europe and it stretches between the Basque provinces of Soule, Basse-Navarre and Navarra. It is a very rich forest with a remarkable fauna and flora. It abounds in stags, deer and wild boars. Certain bird species, for example the whitebacked woodpecker, live only in this part of the Pyrenees. In the autumn the undergrowth is rich in mushrooms and boletus, or cepe, in particular. It is also during this

season that a large number of migratory birds fly over the Basque cols. Birds of prey like harriers, kites or the spectacular ash-grey cranes use these cols, lower than those in the neighbouring High-Pyrenees, to reach their winter quarters in southern Spain or in Africa.

South of the natural barrier of the Pyrenees the rains are much rarer and because of this the landscape is more Mediterranean. Holm oaks, cork oaks as well as olive trees are the most common trees here and there are a great number of rabbits and hares. In this landscape the rivers have cut deep gorges, called "foz" in Spain, in the limestone. These steep cliffs are a refuge for big birds of prey. Vultures, eagles and falcons use these rocks to build their nests. If you can still admire these vultures today, it is partly thanks to a very active pastoralism. These immense birds are carrion-eaters and they only eat dead animals which is why their survival greatly depends on sheep dying in accidents or from illness. Through their obvious role as mountain "cleaners" they are much appreciated and respected by the shepherds.

In the extreme south of the Navarra the landscape change into a real desert.

This extremely arid region is called Bardenas. The landscape is impressive with its completely eroded cliffs and its dried-out riverbeds. The only animals living here are adapted to the desert climate. Some birds, like the pintailed sand grouse, are the same as the ones living in the Moroccan desert.

THE ROADS TO SANTIAGO DE COMPOSTELA

Santiago de Compostela cathedral

Ostabat

James the Greater, Jesus apostle, evangelized the Iberian Peninsula. When he returned to Jerusalem he was beheaded by order of Herode. A boat holding his body was carried by the winds and is said to have stranded on the beaches of Galicia. Forgotten for eight ceturies his bones were recovered thanks to the dream of a hermite who was guided by a rain of stars to the place that was to become Compostela, "field of stars". A pilgrimage in 813 marks the start of the christians' reconquest of Spain from the Muslims. The Bishop of Cluny was the first French pilgrim and he laid out the first route. This pilgrimage ended in the 15th century when the wars of religion started.

Saint Jean-Pied-de-Port, the Saint James door

Hundreds of thousands of pilgrims flocked to Santiago de Compostela every year despite the difficult journey, the changeable weather, hostile regions to go through, the brigands, rutted trails and paths, few bridges and the fords where they had to put their trust in the ferrymen.
Aimery Picaud, a monk from Poitou, wrote the "Guide for Compostela pilgrims" giving details of the itineraries to follow, the sanctuaries to venerate, the hospices and places to avoid.
Stone crosses marked out the routes.
The pilgrimage was a heaven-sent manna for every town the pilgrims went through. It led to the creation of businesses, churches, hospices and brotherhoods. Frankish quarters were established in many Spanish towns to receive the pilgrims travelling from France. French abbeys opened many establishments. Artisans settled in the towns and a mix of cultures brought a new cultural richness.
Monastic and Hospitaller orders opened hospices ; the richest, the hospitallers of St John of Jerusalem and the Knights Templars, gave the pilgrims not only moral support but also material assistance like loans etc.
Most of the pilgrims in the Middle-Ages came from the wealthy classes and this is why the towns they passed through greatly benefited ; some pilgrims even gave all their possessions to different orders.
The pilgrim is recognisable thanks to his big pelerine cape, his wide-brimmed hat, his scrip (bag), his flask made from a colocynth and his pilgrim staff with ferrule.

On arrival in Santiago the pilgrim was given a shell which he proudly wore as a proof of the accomplishment of his pilgrimage.
The English and Nordic ships sailed to Bordeaux or Bayonne where the pilgrims disembarked.
The main land routes went through Tours, Vézelay, Le Puy and Arles.
The first three join at Ostabat and continue via St Jean-Pied-de-Port. Going through Arles the pilgrims would pass Toulouse, the Somport and Sanguesa cols. All the routes then join up in Puente la Reina and the remaining 700 kilometres to Santiago de Compostela are called "camino frances".
The coastal route from Bordeaux first went through the dangerous and deserted landscape of the Landes and then continued via Bayonne, San Sebastian, Zumaya, Bilbao and Oviedo, or Vitoria.
It wasn't until the 20th century that the pilgrimage started again. It is still made today, but under very different conditions.

Pilgrim

CANTABRIA
BIZKAIA
Bilbo/Bilbao
GIPUZKOA
Donostia
San Sebastian
ÁLAVA
Vitoria-Gasteiz
NAVARRA
Iruñea/Pamplona
LABOURD
BASSE-NAVARRE
SOULE
ESPAÑA
FRANCE
LA RIOJA
Logroño
CASTILLA-LEÓN
ARAGÓN
Bayonne
Biarritz
St-Jean-de-Luz
Hendaye
Irun
Tolosa
Eibar
Arrasate Mongragón
Estella-Lizarra
Tudela
St-Jean-Pied-de-Port
Mauléon-Licharre
St-Palais
Miranda de Ebro
Calahorra

TABLE OF CONTENTS

Design
Erick Garcia – Frédéric Thouand

Texts
Alain Pagoaga

Photographic contributors
Patrice Blot - Pierre Guy Edgard Rosa - Jean Jacques Gelbart - Philippe Laplace - Cédric Mesplés
Marc Moranne - Alain Pagoaga - Stéphane Semper - Frédéric Thouand - Jacques Thouand
Oxocelhaya caves - Musée Grévin - Toros y Moscas

Photographic reproduction
Profilkolor - Biarritz

Printed in the EU
FISA - Barcelone

Federico Feria

Collection of Editions THOUAND – BP 173 – 64204 BIARRITZ (France) - T. 33 5 59 41 26 10
http:// - e-mail :

Copyright May 2006 – Printed in April 2006
ISBN 29516649-6-6